Get Ready!

Are you an ambitious, determined, and sassy black woman? Then, show yourself some love with this empowering coloring book! Each page is adorned with stunning illustrations that will look even better once filled in by your creativity. But it's not just about artistic expression - each image also comes accompanied by a positive affirmation to remind you of how awesome and capable you are. So as the colors fill up the page, let these uplifting words warmly embrace your soul: be proud of being unique and unafraid to take on whatever life throws at them! So grab those crayons or colored pens for a journey as fun as it is inspiring - have fun while reminding yourself just how amazing YOU are!

AFFIRMATION
I believe in myself and my capabilities because I can achieve anything I set my mind to.

AFFIRMATION

I'm not afraid to take risks and step out of my comfort zone, because that's where my growth and success lie.

AFFIRMATION

I'm developing a strong
work ethic and am willing
to put in the time and
effort to achieve my goals.

AFFIRMATION

My gender does not define my success, and I have the power to break any glass ceiling that stands in my way.

AFFIRMATION

I set clear goals for myself and develop a plan to achieve them because a clear roadmap can lead to my success.

AFFIRMATION

believe in my worth and will not settle for anything less than I deserve.

AFFIRMATION
I surround myself with positive and supportive people who will uplift and encourage me on my journey and I do the same for them.

AFFIRMATION

I am open to learning and growth because there is always room for improvement!

AFFIRMATION

I care for myself physically and mentally because my well-being is crucial to success.

AFFIRMATION

I always cultivate a positive mindset and believe success is possible for me and others.

AFFIRMATION

I celebrate my accomplishments, no matter how small, because they all contribute to my success.

AFFIRMATION

'Il never forget that failure is not the opposite of success; t's part of the journey toward success!

AFFIRMATION

Life is too short! So, I'm willing to take on new challenges, even if they initially seem daunting.

AFFIRMATION

I'm doing today what most people won't, so I can have tomorrow what most people can't!

AFFIRMATION

I'm an authentic original me
and not a copycat counterfeit
of somebody else!

AFFIRMATION

I was created for this moment in time. With God, nothing is impossible!

AFFIRMATION

I am open to new opportunities and experiences and embrace change enthusiastically and optimistically.

AFFIRMATION

I am worthy of love and respect and I treat myself and others with kindness and compassion.

AFFIRMATION

I am grateful for everything
I have and know that more
good things are coming my
way.

AFFIRMATION

I am surrounded by love and support, and I know I can always reach out for help when needed.

AFFIRMATION

I am resilient and have the strength to bounce back from any setback.

AFFIRMATION

I trust in my abilities and
believe that I can
overcome any obstacle
that comes my way.

AFFIRMATION

I trust in my abilities and believe that I can overcome any obstacle that comes my way.